The Holding Ground

Angela Morton

THE COLLECTIVE PRESS

Cataloguing In Publication
Data for this book is available from the British
Library

ISBN 1 899449 90 6

Published with the financial support of the
Arts Council of Wales.

Main Typeface; Arial
Type setting by Anvil
Cover design by John Jones
Original photograph by Angela Morton

Printed and bound in Great Britain by
MWL Digital Solutions, Pontypool.

THE
HOLDING
GROUND

Acknowledgements

Versions of some of these poems have appeared in the following publications: Beyond Bedlam (Anvil Press), Blodeuwedd (Headland Press), Open University Poets' Anthology, The Swansea Review, The Interpreter's House, New Welsh Review, Poetry Wales, Scintilla, Envoi.

Some have been prize winners in the following competitions: Aberystwyth Open, Bridport, Cardiff International, Conwy Festival, York Open.

A page of names would be an insufficient acknowledgement of the many whose inspiration has contributed to bringing these poems into being: the task of making them into a collection has been encompassed through a collaboration with Alicia Stubbersfield, without whose grace and humour and knowledge of the route the journey might well have been abandoned

for John and our family

Contents

The room at the top of the stairs

Stuck with how to do my maths, I'd seek my brother's
help. He'd be upstairs. I'd tap on the closed door; wait
for the answer of his voice.

His room was sprung with tension. Far into the night
he'd toil, his domed brow lined with sweat that lay
like beads of mercury. His smoky room was coiled

about him like the snake I, younger, saw there,
trapped among red tinctures in a 2lb bottling jar;
and in the ashen air, he'd clear

a space for me and patiently assist me to erase
the mishaps on my page. Then I'd return downstairs
and soon be out to play while in his den

his tall, thin, body toiled over his script as number
swarmed up against the light: a clotting throng
cramped to a blackening mass, dulling the glass.

After the wedding day his room became an emptied cell
until the time my father drew the blinds
and passed me red crepe paper and my mother's cycle lamp;

with wizened elastic we hooded it. In the reddening, began
the alchemy of light: how to extract the secret paper
sealed in the black envelope, and later, how to slip it,

trapped air silvering in minute bubbles, through
the invisible caul, into the shimmering pool
held in the white enamel bowl. It wavered

in the reeking dish, as he taught me how to count
time's tremor. *Higgledy piggledy one, higgledy
piggledy two, higgledy ... nine,* we chanted

as, in the fluids' wash, tree, sky and field, cloud,
leaf and vein took up their outline, breathed
into form, and all their glowing colour

silvered to white and was distilled into
the glistering of black's infinities. Breathing
in unison, we scaled the measurements of time

and in an hourglass I saw how love and time
lay, intertwined, in the dark room where lapping water-light
trembled; trembled,   at the approaching ebb.

The word nobody thought they said

I don't remember how I knew Daddy had nearly
died. You'd drawn a damp green and forbidding
ring around the room where he lay wrapped on your
wide bed. Aged nine, I know it's dangerous,
to others and yourself, to step inside a livid
ring that's darkening the field's most secret folds;
have learned, already, how sometimes danger
lurks in magic places; and the fairies
sometimes will fail to make all well.

I did not cross your damp green line, stayed
numbly on the landing; listened for the mumble
of his breath, as you climbed the stairs
with all those clinking trays, and crossed in
and back and in. I dared not risk
the harm my step-across might bring and, half-
breathing, stayed there till the danger in the room
had stopped coming out a bit and
the air was easier to have.

I was so frightened, that morning when you
led me in to see him again, and he looked
so very tired and sad
as if some wand had touched his forehead,
his cheeks, his weary eyes, his tender mouth.

If you avoided saying it to me then, that forbidden noun
I had known it already, from my fairy tales: that word they use
when people fall into the kind of sleep
from which even their wife and little daughter, all
those they love, can't ever rouse them.

Sea sorrow

1 *Miranda*

Before the tempest, she'd curl small,
nesting in the warm shape her mother left;
so close, she felt the movement of his heart.

She'd watch his lips work silently
over his solemn book and tell the words
he could not give to her,

his female child. Yet under oath
he has disclosed the guarded drawer,
shown her the gilded robes, amazed her

with the rush of cardinal and azure;
lifted the tissues,
let her touch the hems.

But then she'd heard the vessel of his heart,
murmuring. She'd watched the tide and known
how it might drown.

Later, she learns to read
the line he walked,
so delicate, along the margin

of her path; for his voice
was in her babble, helped shape
her earliest play of breath

and throat. Triumphantly, vowels
flowered on her tongue:
ear's drum

beat to his cadences
as he spread
the white and saffron cloak

and let her ride.

2 Prospero

I heard the seas turn slippery. Breakers
cleave and flatten, pleating under
undertow as they dress your mother

in their weeds: wrack
tangles her; combs hair
with salt till all is spoil:

our boat is prised
adrift and you
who had thought my craft

protection for whatever came,
are left as salvager.
I did not let you learn how frail

my voice had grown.
Less than five fathoms deep
I wait: no pearl nor coral,

only the trace of ribs
in border soil.
I lost

Miranda, lost you,
cried for you as I died

for you in grief and love my white bones flute.

The swallow

This morning as the swallows gather,
and poise on the power wires,

I have forgotten the official reason
for the cause of death. There are no

words, Latin or otherwise, that can
account for it. All those long years

when her shocked mind and body tried
and tried again to piece the fragments

shattered by convulsive treatment and
the news of his stopped heart.

Again the swallows gather and poise on the power wires and the barn roofs
thrum with tribal rhythm as a feathered clan prepare for embarkation
to a homeland for which there is no map except that silvered one
secreted in the heart and in the bone.

The moth

Looped to her dusty wardrobe rail
is this disintegrating ribbon, in crumpled
mauve, that once was threaded through a disc
of compressed camphor crystals: there
it hung, to baffle flitting moths. Seasons
long-past, have folded up her silks;
have sold the furs whose glistening darks
she'd hug across her shrinking breasts

as though no thought of a heart that ceased
to beat, might pad across her mind

as she, luxuriously, shrugged on
the perfume of the pelt; or the fear
of how a disguised moth

might infiltrate the latched interior
bringing in
a must of crumbling wings
no camphor could erase.

The closed drawer

I have forgotten what glove size fitted
your hand. Your wardrobe opened to reveal
the rows of size four shoes, like harboured

boats, the floaty chiffon scarves, the special
smell, the drawer for gloves rolled in their
pairs. One day long after you had gone,

my fingers touched a little pouch
of softest kid: a glove rolled with a spray of lavender,
at the back of a closed drawer. I brought it

out into the light. I couldn't contract my palm
enough to squeeze it on: blue of midnight, a tunnelling
elbow length, with delicately trellised slits;

light as a swallow's bones.

When our mother turned away

In the tall garden where they had seen
a swing for you, I lurch and
learn to catch the ball
your father throws.

On that smoothed lawn I
drew breath, ran, and swung: ate
from the tree which they had planted
when they set your seed.
You were someone secret;

something they could not name,
might never tell to me: until the day I glimpsed
their gleam, those pearls. Set like a crescent moon
unseen they'd lain so long, in their velvet box, the clasp
cold, but starred with minute jewels.
They were a husband's gift, when gifts and words
had lost their powers.

Letting them fall like a flower, at last she told
how you came to her
and how, when all

was still; the midwife broke
the silence of the room. *He's perfect,*
this little boy. Quite perfect. Won't you
even look at him?   Unmade,

the mother turned her face
away: *too cruel.*   She could not see
how tender were the woman's hands
as she laid you in the muslin sheet,
drew up the hem fine-sewn
with snowy lace.

Though we've no
name for you, you run and babble
in our dreams:

as our mother watched me move,
always there was a love within
for her still born

who did not leave a spoken scar,
did not even once disturb the air,

but always ever were.

At Llangenny Falls

My brother, on the far side of the weir,
is veiled with spray in this October light
while Salmon leaping through the pulse of air

defy the swirling wall; hurl a furled fear
of stunned home-ground, against the river's height.
My brother, on the far side of the weir

has gone beyond our call.   Could he still hear
Usk's tall crescendo, would he still delight
in Salmon leaping : through the pulse of air

has his heart turned aside? Is he elsewhere
while homing fish arc fast, in glistening flight?
My brother, on the far side of the weir

moves among darkening trees. As colour silvers, here,
has his heart lost rhythm : tuning with the plight
of Salmon leaping through the pulse of air?

Across hurt years, these currents shift and wear;
soon all the shining shadows burn to white:
my brother on the far side of the weir ---

the Salmon, leaping, through the pulse of air.

The long mirror

1 The shining flower

Do you remember when you brought in
the miniature Iris in its plastic pot? Its roots
already parching in neglected soil,
we soaked it in the ward's washbasin
while a nurse fetched a kitchen saucer
to hold the moisture
in. Before you left we placed
the tender plant on my cramped locker;

there it shone for me as it revived
among the primroses and shaky rows
of cards and messages, *Iris
Reticulata*, the netted bulb;

it did not live long
in our muffled air.

Now, I'm at home among earthed
Irises, and see the purple robes,
their sprinkle of lit gold
upon the tongue,

and my heart
undoes the years, returns me
to that harsh interior,
that desert interlude:

the small, secreted, nets,
the rows of beds and lockers,
the rigours of that winter;

the courage of the shining flower.

2 My mother's glass

I loved the smell of lavender
as it came into the room,
the noise the hinge made,
like a quiet shout
when she opened wide
her wardrobe door

and I saw another bedroom
swinging in the mirror.

I'd watch as she'd adjust
a pleat or hem line, smooth
a freshly ironed blouse
across her ample breasts.

Now, she's so long
somewhere else that cautiously
I press the catch and her tall glass
swings wide:

at first it's misted
as if a breath, breathed
more than a generation past
had misted it

then it's reflecting images
of narrow beds
in a room that's heaving with
the heavy breaths of strangers:

this is a bedroom scene we've each
had to inhabit. Anxiously I wonder
at the complexity of each inheritance

and what I should learn from the bleak pattern
of those narrow beds,
the double row of lockers, drawers that
jammed, clothes that belonged to
someone else we'd been once
but before the sickness came to us

The holding ground

Love is the holding ground. There is no
other, as grass grows grey as skies
and her thinning body has become too heavy
to walk the quiet lane alone:

there is no other, as she lies, rigid,
in the bed they'd shared; as she sits, unmoving,
while the phone is ringing; as she stands
in unlit rooms, or, motionless, pressed
to the cold glass, stares out
at silence; through the star less night, stares,
searching for the headlights of the car:

there is no other, as she envies
Jennifer for her accomplished
end; her mind
turns on a razor's edge
as she traces the vein's flow
along her inner arm and the blue map
on the skin below her palm:

love is the holding ground, as she attempts to calculate
the properties of all those pills;
as she tests the strength of blue farm-twine and
eyes the height of the barns' beams;
as she watches the river's course: how near
the edge it thrusts its current down;

love is the holding ground,
there is no other as she dreams
seas of enveloping waves :

all these, and more
than these, my mind hovered over,
over and over but always stalled before
accomplishing the finished picture

until I, in a phase of hideous clairvoyance,
witnessed the method I had already used
and the opening door as you
came in upon raw red.

Love is the holding ground; there is no note,
no letter that could atone for such betrayal;
each time you left the house, I knew I could not
kiss goodbye
and then go on to do this to us

love, there is no other.

Evidence

"Do you like snow" says this dark
one. Young and slim, she has a quiet
beauty quite out of place with the place

I am in, sitting in that sweltering
doctors' side room on a vinyl chair
my sticky skin is being sucked to

while on the far side of the glass
those quiet stars of ice are freely falling

I could not answer, and she took for 'No'
my silence as I remembered frozen water-light
frosted stars' light, and underneath the glassy

buzz of fluorescence, tried to imagine
moonlight; tried to remember
how the moon's light was

while on the dull side of the glass
dissolving shards of loss are falling

Against her dusky skin the slim dark doctor
wore blouses of pale silk
and looked so elegant and neat
I had seen through her plot:

she is a lawyer:
she is busy getting marriages annulled:
she is setting patients' husbands free:

as all the while outside the glass
dissolving plumes of snow are duly falling, falling

and then I glimpsed how more than thirty years of troth
might have become as insubstantial as a beam of moonlight moving silently
across our roof, our window panes, the summer grasses

Watching the crows

I sit below these castle walls
and watch: watch how the crows,

and the shard-shadow of these hoards,
black swoop; swoop back, devouring:

am fired with gratitude
to see those black-fucked vampires

today are simply
crows.

Day release

and the journey hard
to believe. Each turn in the lane
veering to home. Yet so soon

winter's sun fading, the afternoon
spent. And soon the nurses
are asking, *Did you have a nice*

time Angela?   A nice visit
home?   I didn't tell them
what the light was like

as I stepped under our lintel;
how in the kitchen our yowling cat
in recognition wrapped and pressed

his furry warmth against my feeble legs.
I keep the dapple
of these memories to hold against

that moment in our bedroom when I glimpsed
the imprint of the separated person; the cold
hot-water bottle's rib

marking a rumple
in the place where once we had lain warm.

Mercurial fields

One moon-loomed night, in that lit flood, electric
powers seemed to roam abroad and dance
and prance about the wards.   I'd lolled and flopped
against the madhouse walls, a pale rag-doll,
compliant with the madhouse rules, but on that upset
moon-hit night some other magnetism veined the ether
and caused the river from its bed to rise mercurial;
that night something outside my weird thin wired self
attracted me: commanded and insisted *Go*
Go. GO. Do not look back but GO.

In dreams so many times I'd set out on the journey home
and viewed the maps through a crazed lens;
in drug disordered dreams so many times had ploughed
those Escher furrows and their convoluted fields

had found on the out side exists a labyrinth for which I have no
guiding thread. Out there vast trees upraised to the windy skies
are coiled about with snakes. Are those trip wires exposed beyond
the iron of the gates? And the heart's maps, that without sight inform
the brain of the way home? Scrambled and smelted down.

But yet the command insisted *Go*
Yes Go. Do not look back. Rise
from your seat. Extend beyond E8. Hold tight
as you descend. As if your slippers press on broken eggs,
creep past the inside window on the lower ward. Avoid the gazes
of the drowned. At last unlatch
the outer door.

On the out side and all about
is the spread night
and the frayed ribbon of the road. Outside
is the moon, whose presence
in this place, is only seen and known through glass.

Behind my back, still, were the attractions
of the fields of home as I, paced by a nurse, was led
back to the ward, the dormitory, my narrow bed.
Beyond me was the journey,

the blackened patterns of the constellations,
night-cries of homing birds, the lures
of silence-feathered owls.

A visitation on the path

When, like her tongue, her talk
was dried to dust, and all her sound was clamped
inside her mind, and day by day
by day they took their speechless walk
along the path that led to Pwll y Wrach,
bad thoughts

conspired to thrust a weight
across her shoulders

but there came, he told her after, a sudden moment
when he felt the silence in her
start to stir, and rift,
as on the path she stopped. Slowly
she shifted her thinned body
across a boundary and stooped down
to the earth; and then she

spoke: *Look,* she said,
look where I've seen, and in her palm
there shone, newly fallen,
a small feather -- this was the first sign:

and they went on, and day by day her mind
began its slow releasing.
She watched how trees began their shimmer;
saw the bend of coming summer grasses
as they sheened in the winnowing wind

and then she knows how clear the birdcall is,
how keen the distant falls; she feels air's
stir, as she witnesses the water's nimbus
as it rises and
disperses from its sharp pitch
of sighing stone, down. Down, down deep
into the silenced dark of Pwll y Wrach, touching
the meniscus of the verdant cauldron, shining
within the weird alembic
of the witch's pool. On and on she moves
towards the water's fall of filtered light, a sun stream

as dust motes churn, and, feather fine,
the countless atoms
chime into the sun. Grace notes

rise from the fall, and calm.   As if
some feathered form
she'd later come to recognise
approaching silently
had raised some sorrow from her shoulders.

On the brink

In the vast kingdom of the dispossessed
we were attended even in the bath, where they'd
shampoo my clotted locks. One
drew them out in lengths along my brush, a second
wielded a hair dryer; my scalp was scraped
by metal grips. All was too hot, too

heavy; limp as those stagnating stems of
keeling flowers in the dayroom vases, as
in sagging bedroom slippers yet another day I sat;
sat at the window watching the tall trees, how the light

moved through their leaves. When
starved hair had creased itself into a straggle,
I was taken through a maze of
echoing corridors and was led beneath the weight of
gurgling pipes to a small airless place, hotter even
than the dayroom; a basined, mirrored
cubicle that jabbered Radio One
and smelled of something burning, reeked
cheap perfume and hissed and steamed with
sulphurous chemicals. At the next basin
hunched an ancient woman whimpering and
crying for her mother.

The hairdresser was tee shirted and chatty but I
couldn't tell her what I wanted. The old woman was
still crying as they combed the scanty tufts from her pink scalp,
then skewered and twisted and fixed them with clips.
In my steamy closet mirror as it ran tears
I glimpsed a heavy door bang to a close
as the bright scissor-jaws snapped and
chipped against the comb. With each sharp
crunch, my hair dropped from me, mounding

and shrivelling in my lap and heaping
silently around my chair. A broken broom
came stealthily across the tiles to claim it
and I saw the brown coils tangle and then
mingle with the old woman's bristly clippings.

Back on the ward, I sat, and watched the empty
trees. As passing nurses said how nice
my clipped hair looked, I attempted to forget
the black and white crazed floor,
my rag of hair as it was being swept towards
a pile of dust.

Then you were there. You
helped me into my blue jacket

and we went out to the woods, and found
our waterfall beyond

and I forgot about my hair
as you took my hand and said,

Look how the trees
are poised right on the brink of Spring.

The trolley

Always in pairs, those nurses in charge of this weird chariot ---
this tiered box on wonky wheels that has within its hold
those multitudinous incarnidines
of space and time and grace and place: Pandora's
tricky box of side-effects and goodies for the weary weird.

Like airline pilots on a complicated mission
or those pairs that zapped and sped towards a 999,
one for the casualty, one to control the speeding vehicle
(ours on E8 was way out past
its sell-by date) it took the both of them to
kick-start it and somehow coax and wheedle it
to pride of place. It was the dayroom centrepiece.

At the appointed time (approximate) it would appear, careering in
on unsafe wheels (an out-of-kilter Safeway trolley) as the nurses
strained to tame it to its squealing halt.
Its painted chest was locked and barred, the key worked
doubtfully. But, finally, they'd open up the double hinge and flap it down
as if it was an ice cream bar, at which the better
patients stood in queues. Always, one nurse stood guard.
They had a pile of charts, a list of names, hers and his and hers
mumbled like charms as, into gnome-sized plastic cups, like pebbles
in a beach-bucket, they heaped a pharmacopoeia. *Take these
for me please Angela* they'd say, tipping
the doctors' dolly-mixture quota for today into your sweating palm,
Take these for me they'd say, as if this incantation
bestowed some charm upon a dayroom filled with breaking minds.

All processes reversed, the ancient trolley sealed,
and veered back to the place from whence it came, the ritual
ceased. A sturdy chain was passed across its body
and then fastened to the wall. Such omni-potency, such powers
filed and held in a contraption of chipped paint; and chained

precious as the ancient manuscripts I witnessed once
a world away, in Florence: the library at St Lorenzo:
a place inhabited now only by ghosts. All passes

so also this great edifice: day rooms, side-rooms and hairdresser's basins,
kitchens, groomed grounds, and chapel and laundry, *all*
the great globe inhabits start to disintegrate: a weird diaspora
of nurses, patients, trolls and trolleys, doctors' scripts and flower beds.

The other day I met again a man who once with shining spoon
posted parcels of processed meat through my lost mouth.
Now he's gone and got a job outside; *it's all a ghost town*
up there, was what he told me,
turning his day's load of deliveries across our rutted lane.

As bedlam eased

One day as Spring began to ease
and it grew warm, we walked again
beside the stream and in a hidden place
lay down again among the thrusts of green;

but I was fearful that my clothes
might mesh with tell-tale twigs and grass,
and I was fearful of the darkness
in my thin body's house

as quietly we lay in one another's green
beneath the circling leaves
as when from far, but near, unseen
the moon moves quietly among the waves.

By what it was

We're scarred, us both,
by what it was
when I was in the wilderness:

tissues of married flesh
marred and scared, begin
to make again

across the trough of time that's burned
into remembrance.   Our tried
and tired minds have separately drawn

a difficult and different map.
Now, each by each, we trace
these treacherous currents

as this sloe-black river
with its silt
desert-dried and cruel as sand

assaults the veined and
reddened sight --- comes in
stinging when the wind's unkind.

A foolish thing to say a sorry sight

My dearest chuck, Duncan comes here tonight.
" And when goes hence? "   Tomorrow,
as he purposes.   Of course

we know, bone-deep, we know tomorrow and
tomorrow, Duncan will not return: blood-deep,
ambition croons within the discourse
of the crones, coursing the marrow.

Blood-deep, alas, these players: this performance
is outsized and over-pitched: where sorrow
should have welled, insistent as a sneeze, a giggle
farts; red ketchup's rife, and gore
pours at the feast where Banquo
creaks, in all too solid flesh. *Out, out,*
damned spot (the stain said hot
but the label said not) *My Lord is often*
thus (surely, the bard did not intend
this thus)   Macbeth wades on

as one by one his henchmen fall, props
fall, the tacky battlements .... all,
all with a dying fall
while stifled mirth tiptoes the aisles: *birth-*
strangled babe ---   and yet:

yet even as this unhappy cast turns feast
to gall; even as, with relief,
we watch the curtain fall
on murdering ministers; even now,
something is won:

not even this play's run could bodge
it all
        still, Burnam Wood, unstoppable,
is come to Dunsinane. Yet

light thickens, while
a pitchy crow makes way
to the rooky wood

and thus begins the play of elm
around the singing bowl
the stir

of language tuning,
turning and chiming at the rim

Amid the word

In this dawn hush I watch the blossoming
of wood, and let my humming brush describe
smooth circles in small pools of wax;
then let the flex play out and then

recoil.   Perfect recall. Kick off my shoes
and plant my feet and let the weight
ply out around me, tautening my waist: aerobics
at Selwyn College library! At 821 ENG. LIT.
I arch my feet and hustle on past 228 THEOLOGY
guiding my *Constellation* (per ardua
ad astra) with the ease I learned
with pushchairs and with loaded prams.

At the threshold now, I nudge my naked heels
into the sisal mat and tease the fibres
causing them to yield
the debris they have plucked from busy shoes:

then, through my heels, remembering
the needled walk past Clyro church,
I know

how the high shoulder of the hill
with cream-fleeced sheep in sprung relief, looms
as an arras

and clear, in my mind's
ear, hear the white-rimmed, broad-brimmed Wye,
her lilt and ring on silt and stone at Hay;

and the smell of living water,
and the fronded scent of bracken, drifts
amid the wax, and the fresh of newly printed texts.

Now the first reader has arrived. It's time
to gather up my drone
and lift my brushes, heavy as a sleepy child,
upon my practised hip; leave
the swept and polished hive, and make
for my own word-work:

upstairs, I tap
the keys, press out
the words
potent as Braille.

Their power pierces my meridian:

Yn y dechreud
In the beginning

Y creodd Duw
God created

Y nefoedd a'r daear
the heaven and the earth.

A Duw a welodd mai da oedd
And God saw that it was good.

Dervish

Seeking the still point in the turning world
voluminous in heavy skirts

one foot a pivot into the salt of the earth
it's how it happens, it happens how it is

seeking the still point
in the turning

returning in the turning
seeking the still

along the arteries of the upraised arm
is a river of power from the moon, sun and stars

as light and dust and heat, the whirl of all the stars
travel the body's span

blue of the virgin gown
emeralds of diaphanous insect-wing

as grass and insect wing and an eternal blue
are whirled to gold on gold

and gold's distil
distils to white

it's how it happens,
it happens how it is

skirt and heart and spirit and soul
is, shaman-spiralling

it's now it happens
as now is spiralling within the turn

pivot of the still small star
it's now it is

now
is   is
s

Thomas beside the vaporous Usk

He walks through darkness as the vaporous light
begins to sliver, and coruscating blood
quick-silvers through the veins, lit by the weight

of Mercury. For Mercury has entered;
silvering the white. Crows fly the rooky wood.
He walks through darkness as the vaporous light

lifts from the waters of the Usk and sweat
divides the spine-plumes of twinned swans. As blood
quick-silvers through the veins, lit by the weight

of this last act; then dream and hooded fate
combine in Thomas Vaughan. Full flood,
he walks though darkness as the vaporous light

courses from nostrils to the curious heart.
Enjoin me here ! Bright Mercury inbreeds:
quick-silvers in the vein. *Lit by the weight*

of my intent, Veni ! Conjuncte advenit !
As male and female deliquesce in deed,
he walks, through darkness. As the vaporous light

begins to coalesce, the candle of the night
burns in Usk's waters as the noonday heat:
quick-silvers in the veins: lit by the weight,

suffuses all his wildest dreams of good.
As gleaming Usk saddens to blackened woad,
he walks. Through darkness: as the vaporous light
quick-silvers through the veins: makes light of weight.

The swan of Usk

Brown river waters of the Usk
inexorably

took him further
from the source ... the lost

first place
while the warm drift

of innocent waft from childhood orchards,
wide glimmer

of pure fields,
lifted and lit his dreams.

But adult plumage
tars below the breast; such sorrow
to know the flint of civil war; how
culpable men are.

Each sharp day
exacts a toll.

His brother
is no longer at his side: grief's pall

draws down his head;
topples his questing neck into an arc;

the spray of blossom
yields and scatters on the tide;

under his hidden webs, the waters
sully and mesh;

yet supple with light
he shuttles the darkening weft,
drawn by calm fields beyond the weir
their endless radiance.

Wheatfield under threatening skies with crows

Auvers sur Oise, late summer.
I am working like one actually possessed ...
like someone who meant to commit suicide
and finding the water too cold,
struggles to regain the bank.

See how this artist's sky translates the turbulent turquoise
beneath encroaching black. What might have been
the spinning yellow of his sun, becomes a tree
eclipsed by fevered blue and, to the left, spread-winged,

the gathering crows. Dark, scumbled skies
oppress the orient wheat, the oblique pitch of stalk
has crazed to boiling seas where pitchy crows
fall from tar-feathered skies. Is there, stillborn,

another furious-yellow sun that, threatened,
fails to shine, or burn?   If the eyes traverse
from the left margin to the vulnerable space
the birds of threat have, not yet, overwhelmed,

there, Vincent's cerulean oils have overlaid
the black vee in the heavy sky:
along the centre-fold, the heave of wounded wheat
is flattened by a swathe, a path that climbs a gradient

so slippery no man might follow it to find a gate
and easy sunlight
beyond the torment of the waves,
their restless *pound*
against the sullen, hopeless cliffs.

Don't mock the mocking bird

Come love --- can love close up
those veins whose traces lead to
last year's splintered lanes: lanes
loaded with torn leaves, disrupting

dis RUPT! don't
MOCK! mock-mock

disrupting light: parched lanes
harsh with daft truths, distracting
scarce, good-dark

scarce dark? SCARE
dark!   DON'T mock,
mock-!-
mock--mock

arched lanes brittled with twigs
crackled with mocking birds

Crackled! Cuck old
-old-old. O don't mock
the Mocking Bird
SAD Bird heard only
by the bad bad BAD !

There! it waits. See it sits here; now
here. And here

see ME ! SEE
me down ev
ery road on ev-ery

on every tree down every road in
every wood, it pecks and pecks and
plucks such hurt,

such HURT that blood

blood spits in the throat and

blood sits
in the throat and
THREAT

and threat

threat silts
threat SLITS

and threat . splits . every . word.

Come love

Scum! SCUM!   Come
love, love-love

Come love, and heal those splintered
lanes and ancient boughs creaking
with cackling birds; black grisly
crows that peck slow hurt close
to the soul and to the heart:

come love and cleanse those bloods that lead
to splintered lanes, those wizened trees
cankered with brittled boughs and the mocking
birds' weird cries
heard only by the grossly sad:

come says love *with light and tenderness*
see how, within my glass, those mocking crows
shall be transformed as birds of Paradise.

Dr Gachet and the pale flower

The cloth on which the plant leaves fall
is red and smooth; between the doctor's
thumb and palm is the foxglove

Vincent van Gogh has drawn
as he ached with pigment alchemised
to anguished oils as corn sheaves

burned beneath a fast-dilating sun
and cobalt night revolved within a dome
laser-pierced with spitting light.

Bright as a fresh spilled wound,
the canvas where the flower fades
is a vivid red suffused with blood.

If they were mauve and live
these glove-shaped bells
might stimulate the heavy heart

but Doctor Gachet's flower
pales with a blue
more faded than delphinium, as impulse

held the brush laden with flame,
allowed the blue
to bloom in colour quiet as morphine.

Despair   plucks at a pulse
not where the pigmentation shouts
but where the paint is mute:

the weary pallor
of the doctor; his sad eyes,
the bloodless flower.

Of oak and meadowsweet and broom

They had to send a helicopter
out to get her, so high
this unhinged woman was on those steep cliffs.

Above the Cynfael slopes
she was winched in. Unravelling,

those fraying hems and sleeves
fanned out like ragged feathers

as they swung her in her harness
high across the moon-harshed wastes and chasms
and whitened twists of Avon Gynvael.

That night she was brought down
some say they glimpsed a ragged shadow, vast
it passed over, keening.

Her skinny body seemed to weigh no more
than the frost-faced owl that used to swoop
close to the wards at dusk.

Some say on that June night a hollow voice
was sometimes singing, echoing
and moaning as they took her in.

So wild this chalk-faced woman is, electric
treatment cannot contain her, nor extra
lithium. As the moon increases, up she veers

swooping past those huddled in the corridors
as she swerves against the fastened
windowpanes and utters her cold

Gronw-Gronw! Gronw-Gronw!
as if she summoning and banishing.

One day an old man comes for her.
Someone writes down his name, *Gwydion*
son of Don. As he swears he's the patient's

father, she flares like a bloodied moon
Wife-maker, mother-fucker, claws
at his skin, *bloody, blooded shoddybody. Bloodied*

Bloddy-dyed-wed body. She seizes
his bunch of flowers. One by one
she rips white petals from their stamens.

Eats some. Spits out
the bitter taint. Then knocks and shakes
and strews the country flowers like someone at a opened grave.

Some petals clotted to the clouded surface
of a looking glass, some scattered
like blown feathers down the faceless corridors:

pale tassels of the sessile oak:
the moonlit skin of meadowsweet's drained breasts:
the parted lips of the freak gorse.

When the moon comes into crisis

Some said the moon that night when fully veiled
distilled a vaporous haze as red as blood;

I'd planned to witness this eclipse,
the complete light, its complex gleam so close
to earth; and waking an hour before its time had come
I stepped outside into a waiting world. The air
was powerfully cold, the rising winds
seemed crimped, as if some thing expected
and yet beyond the range of anyone's control,
threaded the atmosphere.

Waiting inside the house for warmth, I must have dozed
for I woke too late, and went outside to gaze
at a face where something
had passed over:
                        missed out, was my first thought
as I walked across the usual morning grass,
and stayed while the moon's light pearled, and then dissolved
as sunrise lit the skies beyond our trees:

mysterious as healing is, while I was unaware
some influence had passed over

as, when the moon comes to a crisis,
like a caduceus, its aureole
touches these roofs and roots, houses and grasses,
needing no witness and no awareness
sometimes to spring a miracle within us.

Living with this

Yes, let us confess it, there's an alchemist who lives
inside me; has made herself at home there, crouched
in my mind, sprawled in my spirit, scrawling her spells
across the sinews of my heart. When she is roused
I call her *Gela,* with a G that's fiery and gutsy: G
as in *Goneril;* for, as the fit is seized on her,
she will transmute my gold through fire-touched red
into rampaging metals; or else
she'll gather up the sum of all my good
and mudden it in greasy phials, then seethe
the disturbed liquor in murky alembics
as with chilled heats and sweaty danks
she summons and conjures

her merciless contractions. Diverse times
my life has suffered from her ravage
but this time I am learning. Fast. Times past
I'd search for exorcists, but now, mysteriously
newly made new again, I've learned it's useless
to try to rid my mind, my soul and spirit
from this alchemist who is an ingrown aspect
of my own.   And so today, while she lolls
peaceably about our shaken house, I'll dance,
and sing to her; and with a gentle G, I'll call her
Gela, as in how you say my usual name.

Pall

When a cold sky's mercury
is sealed with glass,

in the shivering grasses
I hear my sorrow

as it, lonely,
crosses the frozen furrow

and all those separated stars
of snow

on melancholy falls of snow,
is all, all
all these mirrors show.

Isca

it passes, with its stabbing constellations
of momentary star-drops, this same river
flowing through the arc of Llanfaes bridge
and on through summer meadows lush with cattle,

meandering past Llansantffraed where Henry Vaughan
each morning walked in his devotions
with the word: learning a language and a
catching of the rhythm's breath to

speak the incandescent moment, out of time,
when the turquoise of the peacock's feather
is iridescence; blazes
fired with fire.

Web

Lustrous as moonlit cloud,
the early mist has pressed a veil

against our glass. No glimpse
of this morning's boundaries, only a taste
sharp apple cored, until

as its pearl dissolves,
plain light sings in our unshuttered rooms.

As this September day raises a far horizon,
my son calls me to witness, where the struck elm
still stands,

a host of lace:

between each arch, each space, each
twig span, the spiders' threads
have laced a mass of radiant trellises:

wheel and spinning wheel, whirr, blur, ply in
an iridescent skein of shimmered dew,
and then as sun's arc

skims, the bright tree
empties; or so it seems:

unseen, those intricate lattices
like memory's mesh, remain;
but needing certain light to show them.

Though the chance tilt that gave
their sheen, soon masked their print,
we have known them;

their trace remains in us. Quietly now
they lie unlit

while in another season's time, the threaded tree
shines into being:
blazes a spiral track where trails of light

redeem

as faded webs shall spill and glisten
in the vault.

How You Can Help

You can support The Collective by ordering any of their publications from your local bookshop, through your local library or direct from the address on the facing page. The money raised goes back into publishing and supporting poetry.

You can further support poetry through subscription to poetry magazines and by attending poetry readings at venues throughout the UK. Look out for Collective run events or, if you would like one in your area, get in touch with the Events Organiser, address as before.

The Collective

welshwriters.com

The Collective is a non-profit-making organisation formed in 1990 to promote and publish contemporary poetry. Funds are raised through a series of poetry events held in and around South Wales. The backing and generosity of fellow writers is a cornerstone of The Collective's success. Vital funding comes from public bodies including the Arts Council of Wales and donations are often received in support of the movement from members of the public. If you would like to contact The Collective to offer help or support then please write to:

The Co-ordinator
The Chief Editor
or the
Events Organiser.

C/O

The Collective
Penlanlas Farm
Llantilio Pertholey
Y-Fenni
Gwent
NP7 7HN
Wales
UK

fish